www.hants.gov.uk/library

Hampshire County Council

Love YOUR LIBRARY

Tel: 0300 555 1387

SOUTH LONDON TRAMWAYS
1933 - 52

Robert J Harley

MP Middleton Press

Front Cover Picture: On 5th July 1952, bright sunshine greets the last day of South London's trams. Here at the Yorkshire Grey Roundabout, Eltham Green, an HR/2 class car on service 72 has just emerged from Westhorne Avenue. In the background we observe an ex-West Ham car en route to Eltham Church via Eltham Hill. (Electrail Colour Slides)

Rear Cover Picture: London Transport car 1622 has been restored to its full prewar glory. It now resides at the National Tramway Museum in Crich, Derbyshire. Here it is pictured on a crisp winter's day in early 2006. Route 38 once traversed most of South London.

Published October 2006

ISBN 1 904474 89 6

© Middleton Press, 2006

Design Deborah Esher

Published by
      Middleton Press
      Easebourne Lane
      Midhurst, West Sussex
      GU29 9AZ
Tel: 01730 813169
Fax: 01730 812601
Email: info@middletonpress.co.uk
www.middletonpress.co.uk

Printed & bound by Biddles Ltd, Kings Lynn

CONTENTS

INTRODUCTION AND ACKNOWLEDGEMENTS

As a native born South Londoner it has given me much pleasure to assemble this second volume, which covers the London Transport period from 1933 to 1952. Inevitably, the postwar era up to the abandonment of the system has received the lion's share of the street scenes. The challenge was to uncover as many previously unpublished pictures as I could. These rare views show locations now long since vanished under highway improvements or altered by new housing schemes and shopping centres.

Photographs credited in this book include the work of Alan Watkins – by kind permission of Ann Watkins; K.G.Harvie – by courtesy of Pat Chappelle; H.F.Wheeller - by courtesy of Roger Carpenter. Many thanks are due to John Gillham and to Dave Jones of the LCC Tramways Trust for supplying much interesting material from the collections of Roy Hubble, Don Thompson, Norman Rayfield and John Wills. My gratitude also goes to Terry Russell, our resident car drawings maestro, whose work has enhanced many of the previous Tramway Classics volumes.

Readers are reminded that the first volume, entitled *South London Tramways 1903-1933*, covers the early electric era. It features cars operated by the London County Council Tramways. An in–depth study of all metropolitan area lines has been published in the 25 volumes of Tramways Classics centred on the nation's capital. They are listed on the final page.

GEOGRAPHICAL SETTING

The London County Council once administered the area under study. Croydon was situated 'out-county' in Surrey. However, for all practical purposes the town has belonged for many decades in the ambit of South London.

The description 'Inner South London' refers to the postal districts of SE1 and SE11 plus parts of SE16 and SE17. In general, the main roads in this part of London form the approaches to the Thames bridges.

The sections marked South West and South East are self explanatory, although it has to be remembered that a number of SW postal districts actually lie north of the Thames. The tramway termini at Victoria and Chelsea - Beaufort Street, and the route from Putney Bridge to Hammersmith fell into this category.

The area is embraced by a horseshoe shaped upland stretching from Greenwich in the east, peaking at Crystal Palace and tapering down near Clapham Junction in Battersea.

HISTORICAL BACKGROUND

The formation of the London Passenger Transport Board on 1st July 1933 marked a crucial turning point in the history of the capital's tramways. Abandonment of the tram system in favour of 'more up-to-date forms of transport' began in earnest during the mid 1930s. Some short lines such as Chelsea Bridge to Clapham, and Dartford to Wilmington in Kent were replaced by motor buses. However, electric vehicles in the shape of the trolleybus were set to spearhead the conversion of the bulk of the South London network.

Trolleybuses began working from Woolwich to Erith, Bexleyheath and Dartford; they also took over the former South Metropolitan services radiating from West Croydon to Sutton, Crystal Palace and Mitcham. The introduction of trolleybuses on the trunk routes which traversed Tooting, Clapham Junction, Wandsworth and Putney Bridge was planned as but an initial stage before the total elimination of the rail bound vehicles. However, these schemes foundered due to the outbreak of the Second World War.

During the war years trams gave sterling service to South Londoners. Bomb damaged tracks were repaired and many antiquated tramcars were given a new lease of life. There was, of course, no romantic attachment to the trams on the part of the policy makers at London Transport HQ in 55, Broadway, SW1. Post war shortages of new buses only delayed the inevitable, and the conversion scheme resumed in 1950. Diesel buses were preferred to trolleybuses; the whole process was completed on 5th July 1952.

And there the matter rested. The remaining pockets of trolleybus operation in South London disappeared in 1959/60, leaving the field clear for the internal combustion engine. Then a miracle happened – modern trams returned to Croydon at the end of the twentieth century. Their success may just provoke a sustained revival in this traditional and much loved form of transport, so that a second generation of electric traction can again grace some of the South London streets depicted in this book.

INNER SOUTH LONDON
APPROACHES TO THE THAMES BRIDGES

1.   This very familiar scene, recognised the world over, is enhanced by the presence of London trams from the first generation fleet. In the foreground Feltham type car 2133 crosses the points leading to Westminster Bridge. In the early 1950s the presence of tram tracks to one side of the carriageway did not greatly affect the flow of other vehicular traffic. (A.J.Watkins)

2.   Alan Watkins now stations himself on the western side of Westminster Bridge. Car 1840, working service 2 from Wimbledon, approaches the camera. To the left of the tram is County Hall, erstwhile headquarters of the LCC, whilst on the right are the buildings of St.Thomas' Hospital. (A.J.Watkins)

3.   We return to the South Bank in time to witness a convoy of two E/3 class trams on Kingsway Subway service 31 from Wandsworth to Islington. The road layout and the surrounding buildings here at the former junction of Stangate and Lambeth Palace Road have since undergone drastic changes. (A.J.Watkins)

4.   The 1951 Festival of Britain occasioned a complete reconstruction of the approach layout to Westminster Bridge. New conduit track is depicted here on Addington Street. No doubt the motorman of car 1913 appreciates the smooth ride and the chance to 'notch up' to catch the bus ahead! (A.J.Watkins)

5.   The provenance of this very rare prewar view is a mystery. However, the location is not in doubt – Lambeth Palace Road opposite the Houses of Parliament. Former LCC E class car 424 was scrapped in February 1937, some months before the September demise of the western half of service 26 to Kew Bridge. The route from Clapham Junction was converted to trolleybuses. The tracks pictured here continued to be used by a truncated service 26, until this section duly perished on 30th September 1950. Bus route 168 was drafted in as a replacement.

———➤ 6.   We now cross the River Thames to observe trams on the Victoria Embankment. This was the site of an elongated terminal loop for many services, and, although situated north of the river, was always considered an operational part of the South London network. Continuing the theme of rare views, this shot was taken on 21st July 1943 by a visiting American serviceman. Note the anti-blast netting on the windows and the diamond shaped peep holes. The fenders of the tram have been painted white, so that, in theory at least, pedestrians and other road users could identify the oncoming vehicle in the gloom of wartime blackout.
(Anthony F.Tieuli/Terry Russell)

———➤ 7.   Car 1956 reverses on the Embankment, while car 188 waits to take its place on the crossover. Scenes such as these were commonplace during the tramway era, when cheap fares and a frequent, reliable service were taken for granted by the passengers. (A.J.Watkins)

8.	As trams were replaced by buses, the diesel powered invaders encroached on tram territory – quite literally in this case on the Victoria Embankment, where there is precious little room to spare between car 1956 and RTL 957. The latter had supplanted electric traction on the Wimbledon lines. Ironically, bus routes using this thoroughfare were gradually axed in the 1960s and 1970s, so that at the time of writing there are now no regular services at this location. (A.J.Watkins)

9.	The dome of St.Paul's Cathedral looms in the background as car 393, formerly of Croydon Corporation, rounds the curve from Blackfriars Bridge. At peak times there was a car on service 18 every eight minutes; the ride from Purley in Surrey to the Embankment, here in the City of London, was timed at one hour thirteen minutes. How long it would take in today's traffic is anybody's guess! One thing is certain, this whole area is now firmly in the Central London Congestion Charge Zone. (K.G.Harvie)

10.   Back on the south side of the river we encounter E/3 class car 1962 at the junction of Blackfriars Road and Southwark Street. Service 38 to Abbey Wood was a favourite with excursionists. It ran from the centre of town to the county boundary of Kent, where the bucolic delights of Bostall Heath Woods, Lessness Abbey and the windswept marshes on the banks of the Thames offered a much needed change from urban life. (K.G.Harvie)

11.   St.George's Circus, Southwark was one of those fascinating places, where trams seemed to be going in all directions! Sunshine catches car 1991 as it heads south towards Grove Park on service 74. (K.G.Harvie)

Frank Merton Atkins was a distinguished tramway cartographer. Unfortunately, his task of mapping the complete London system was never completed. This is an extract from his 'North Lambeth' sheet. Note that at St.George's Circus there was very little room for tram drivers to manoeuvre. The technique of many a motorman was to increase speed and sail over.

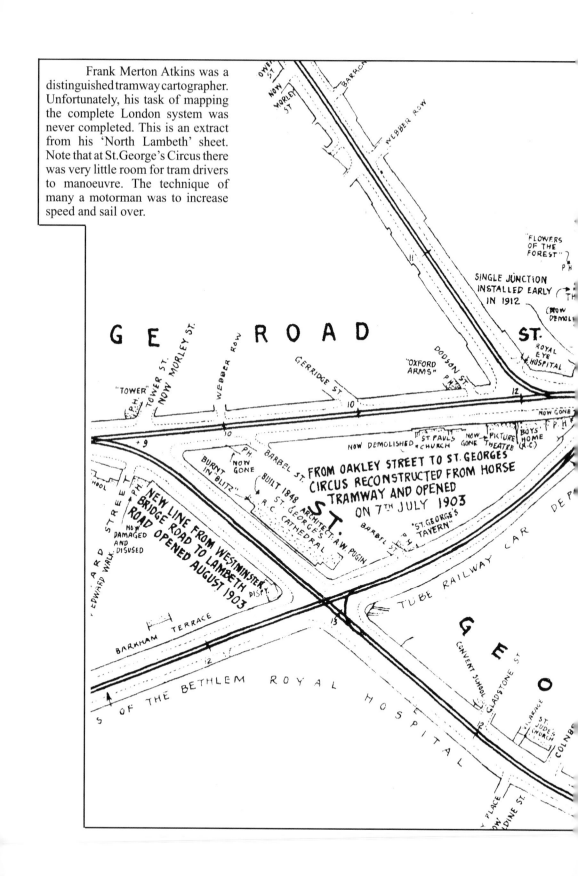

SITE OF DEPOT OWNED BY SOUTH LONDON
TRAMWAY C? AND USED FOR HOUSING THE
HORSES AND LIGHT ONE-HORSE "BLUE" CARS
WHICH WORKED BETWEEN SOUTHWARK
BRIDGE AND NEWINGTON CAUSEWAY

SITE OF
BOROUGH ROAD STN
CLOSED
MARCH 1907

NOW DAVIDGE ST.

MILCOTE ST.

11

12

"SWAN"
P.H.

LIBRARY ST.

GEORGE'S

LIBRARY

B O R O U G H

MILCOTE ST.

LANCASTER ST.

"BRIDGE
HOUSE"

P.H.

BELVEDERE
PLACE

12

S.E. & C. RLY

BRIDGE

P.H.

10

11

P.H.

TRAILING
CROSSOVER

DUKE OF
CLARENCE

MANSFIELD ST.
NOW ROTARY ST.

NOW KEYWORTH ST.

DANTZIC ST.

KELL ST.

BOROUGH
POLYTECHNIC

L

O

N

LANCASTER ST.

THOMAS DOYLE ST.

RCUS

AILING
OSSOVER

FROM ST.GEORGE'S CIRCUS TO SOUTHWARK
BRIDGE ROAD AND SHORT LENGTH IN
LANCASTER STREET
RECONSTRUCTED FROM HORSE TRAMWAY
AND OPENED SEPTEMBER 1904

EARL ST. NOW

ONTARIO ST.

P.H. NOW
GONE

EARL ST.
NOW
THOMAS DOYLE ST.

P.H. "OLD
QUEEN'S
HEAD"

BATH ST.
NOW CONQUEST ST.

GLADSTONE ST.

GARDEN ROW

NOW GONE

BURMAN ST.

NOW MARSHALL GDNS.

MARSHALL ST.

P.H.
"THE
GRAPES"

D

O

N

ST.GEORGE'S MARKET

L.C.C.
ELECTRICITY
SUBSTATION

NOW
CLOSED

SOUTH LONDON
PALACE

DANTZIC ST.
NOW KEYWORTH ST.

KING'S
HEAD
P.H.

9

G
E'
S

GARDEN ROW

BURMAN ST.

"FOUNTAIN"
HALL ST.
MARSHALL GARDENS

GAYWOOD ST.

ONTARIO ST.

"PRINCESS
OF WALES" P.H.

ON ST.

R O A

12.   In August 1950 construction work on
the Embankment caused the rerouting of several
services via Blackfriars Road. Car 1921 coasts
past St.George's Circus round the curve into
Borough Road. (A.J.Watkins)

⟶ 13.   Just a few yards into
Borough Road, car 1921 reverses on the
nearest crossover. Note the splayed tracks
either side of a strategically placed public
convenience. (A.J.Watkins)

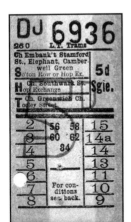

← 14.   The South Bank tram terminus adjacent to Waterloo Station was conveniently situated for travellers wishing to transfer to the railway or the tube. Bearing in mind the volume of today's traffic on Waterloo Road, it is hardly credible that this spot could once have been so tranquil. Car 552 waits before setting out towards Greenwich. (K.G.Harvie)

← 15.   Car 2056 first saw the light of an 'operational day' east of the River Lea in Walthamstow. It seems dwarfed by the Hop Exchange buildings in Southwark Street. This short section was electrified in September 1904, but the proposed connecting link to London Bridge tram terminus in Tooley Street was never constructed. (A.J.Watkins)

16.   Feltham car 2110 stands lone sentinel at Southwark Bridge terminus. This was as far as the tracks went in an attempt to penetrate City of London territory. The encroachment of trams on the famed Square Mile was always a sensitive matter with the City authorities. (A.J.Watkins)

←——— 17.   Car 192 is about to turn left in front of the photographer. The motorman's determined course will be south towards Walworth Road. The Alfred's Head public house on the corner of Newington Causeway stands in the background as almost the only survivor of the wartime bombing. The two starring roles for the central bus department have been allotted to RTL 685 on route 40 and RT 2382 on route 63. Tram service 34 ceased crossing the Elephant and Castle junction on 30th September 1950, to be replaced by bus route 45.   (D.A.Thompson)

←——— 18. At ground level we observe car 1626 on a special to Waterloo Station. Passing in the opposite direction is car 118 on service 56. (K.G.Harvie)

19.   John Gillham very astutely chronicled many street scenes of the late tramway era which were about to disappear for ever. In an age when, if you were affluent enough to own a motor car, you could park your vehicle almost anywhere, there is a leisurely air about this view of the Elephant and Castle. We are looking west from the New Kent Road. It was a fine day on 29th June 1952. (J.C.Gillham)

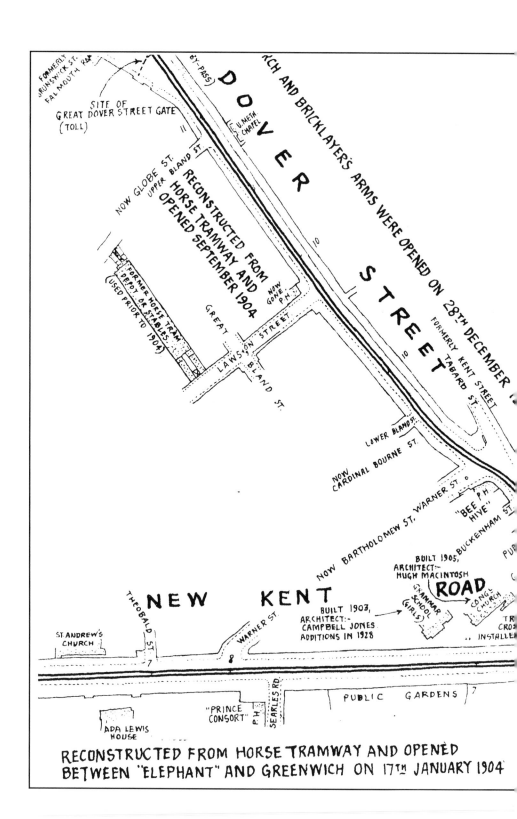

RECONSTRUCTED FROM HORSE TRAMWAY AND OPENED
BETWEEN "ELEPHANT" AND GREENWICH ON 17TH JANUARY 1904

The Bricklayers Arms tramway layout, in many respects a simple junction, once saw a service frequency of over 120 cars per hour.

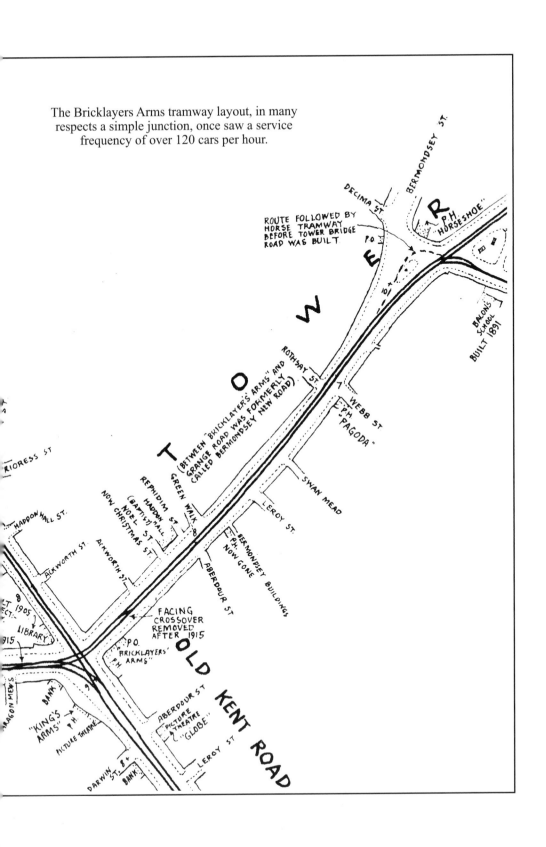

20.   We move a short distance along New Kent Road to arrive at the Bricklayers Arms junction. By the time of this photo the tracks leading off into Tower Bridge Road, to the right of the picture, had been disused for some months. Car 1862, outbound towards Woolwich, emerges from Great Dover Street. (R.Hubble)

———→ 21.   Car 203 rests momentarily outside the Picture House and the Kings Arms at the end of Old Kent Road. Nowadays you would be hard put to recognise anything in this scene. The Bricklayers Arms, like so many other locations featured in this album, has now been entirely 'remodelled' to suit the ever growing demands of the internal combustion engine. (A.J.Watkins)

———→ 22.   Tooley Street terminus lay in the shadow of the wall enclosing the elevated tracks that serve London Bridge Station. Normally the sole reserve of service 70, car 564 on service 68 has somehow managed to get diverted from its more normal course. The eastern terminus for both services was Greenwich. Note the different styles of indicator box on the two trams. (A.J.Watkins)

23.   The 68 acted as a connecting service across inner South London. Car 594 is depicted here in a rare prewar view. Note the splendid condition of the tram with clean bodywork and an advertisement for a product that offers 20 cigarettes for just under 5p! (G.Kemp)

→ 24.   Parker's Row, Bermondsey was typical of many of the bomb damaged streets adjacent to the docks. Postwar reconstruction has already begun as car 572 trundles serenely on to the single track. The whole of this Jamaica Road/Dockhead area has now been completely altered to accommodate a new dual carriageway road. (K.G.Harvie)

→ 25.   Our attention now switches to car 1667 at Victoria. The section of track from Vauxhall Bridge to Victoria was one of the main arteries of the South London system and it survived until the closures of 5th January 1952. On 3rd June 1939, during the last peacetime summer before the Second World War, this tram on service 8 awaits passengers for the round trip to Tooting.

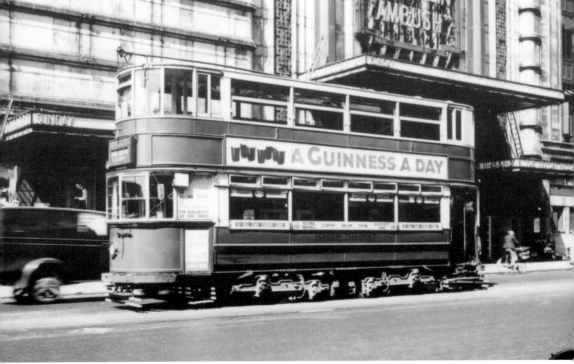

26. The loading islands at Victoria were much appreciated by intending passengers. The motorman of car 1956 waits patiently until the conductor gives him 'two bells' to begin the journey to West Norwood. (A.J.Watkins)

──────▶ 27. Don Thompson was one of the foremost photographers of the London tramway scene. He has positioned himself on Vauxhall Bridge in time to catch car 1880 pursuing a sister vehicle in the direction of Victoria. The trams imposed a lane discipline on such traffic as there was in the early 1950s. With the removal of the rails after 1952 the chaos really started. (D.A.Thompson)

──────▶ 28. In the spring of 1938 the Vauxhall Cross one way traffic layout was constructed to relieve congestion on the approaches to Vauxhall Bridge. A fully illustrated account plus detailed maps is included in companion volume *Victoria and Lambeth Tramways*. Car 160 emerges into Bridgefoot, whilst two private motorists in Austin Sevens of differing vintage line up to attempt to navigate the gyratory system. This tram was unique, being the only E/3 car without trolley poles. (A.J.Watkins)

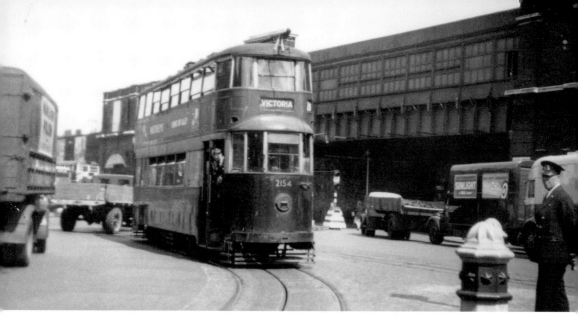

29.   A tram inspector looks askance at the photographer. No doubt he is wondering why anyone should be at all interested in these 'relics of the past' which will soon be cleared from London's streets! The conductor of Feltham car 2154 seems more concerned with an errant lorry that is blocking his progress. (K.G.Harvie)

30.   The date is 20th August 1950. Car 1920 conceals a pointsman, who is about to switch the tram from Lambeth Road back on to Kennington Road. Car 209, working service 12, waits to proceed across the junction. Note the evidence of the Blitz damage to surrounding buildings. (A.J.Watkins)

SOUTH WEST LONDON

31.   We observe Nine Elms Lane, as it was in 1950. The tram tracks in front of car 1927 are bisected by railway sidings leading from the former Southern Railway Goods Depot to wharves on the Thames. (D.A.Thompson)

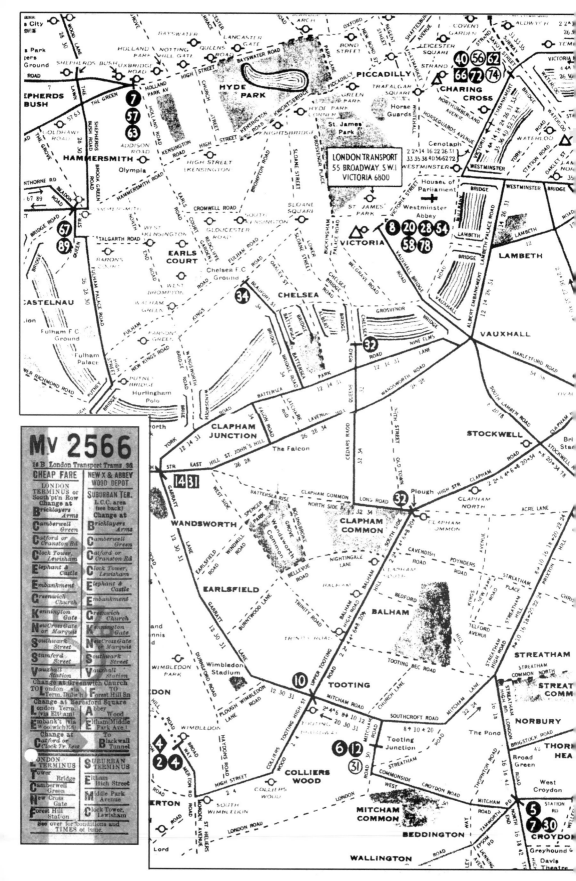

Diagram of tram
services in 1934.

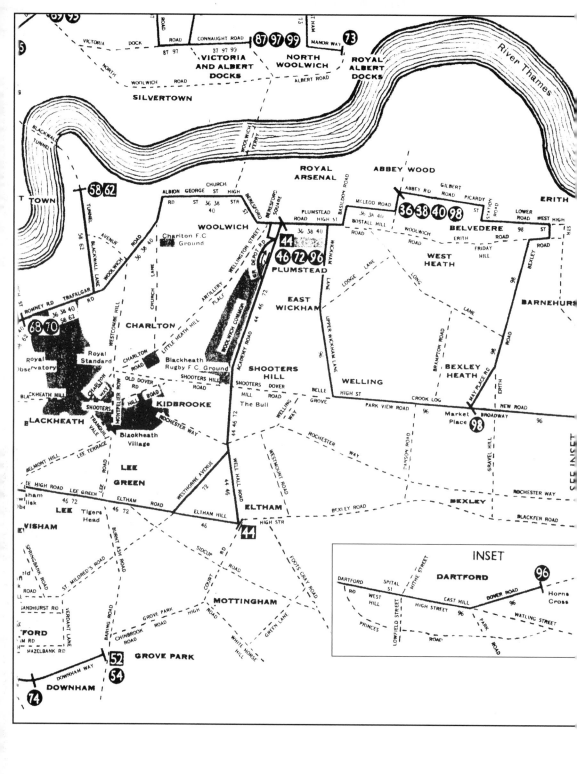

Continuation of the diagram on the previous page.

32. The industrial feel to this part of service 12 was enhanced by the girders that once straddled Nine Elms Lane; the ones behind the camera carried narrow gauge railways from the docks to the gas works. The lines were 2ft/610mm and 3ft/915mm gauge: see Middleton Press volume *Surrey Narrow Gauge*. (A.J.Watkins)

33. Car 1045 is pictured at Chelsea Bridge terminus, just opposite one of the entrances to Battersea Park. Electric traction was inaugurated here on 25th January 1909. Service 32 to the Plough, Clapham was replaced by bus route 137 on 8th September 1937. Luckily, John Bonell arrived just in time to record the scene. Note the substantial waiting shelter for intending passengers. (J.Bonell)

34. Although the rails stopped short of Chelsea Bridge, they did cross Battersea Bridge to reach the terminus at Beaufort Street. An unusual feature was that both tracks were laid very close to the kerb. A tram on service 34 is about to pass a 49 bus en route to Crystal Palace. (A.J.Watkins)

35.   The end of the line at Wandsworth is the setting for two trams - cars 1923 and 1950. The last is particularly appropriate as the date is 1st June of that year. Trolleybus wires were used by route 612; the trams took their power from the underground conduit. (E.Course)

→ 36.   Four trams congregate at Clapham Junction terminus, which was situated in St.John's Hill. The two leading cars are 1594 and 1775. In the foreground the tracks cease. The western section of these tram services was converted to trolleybuses before the Second World War. After 1960 the trolleybuses themselves would be sacrificed. (A.J.Watkins)

→ 37.   The 34 was a tortuous route that practically boxed the compass. A tram tackles the gradient up Cedars Road, where the connecting link to Clapham Common was opened on 26th February 1910. The bend in the foreground was the scene of several spectacular derailments fully described in companion volume *Wandsworth and Battersea Tramways*. (A.J.Watkins)

38.　　At Clapham one of the entrances to the depot was through this 'gap in the houses', as illustrated here. Car 1846 is running into the depot for the last time on 6th January 1951. The following day buses took over.　(E.Course)

39.   On Clapham South Side by The Avenue there was a disconnected turning loop, evidence of which can be observed in the foreground. Many of the properties in this area were very run down after the war, but since then 'gentrification' has struck with a vengeance! (D.A.Thompson)

← ——— 40.   The idea, touted by some so called 'experts', that the roads of South London are lined with buildings of no architectural merit, is disproved by this view. Car 1802 is in Clapham Road, Stockwell by Albert Square. (K.G.Harvie)

← ——— 41.   A little way south of the previous view lies the Swan at Stockwell. Two trams pass by the war memorial clock tower designed by the architect, Frank T.Dear. The lone motorist in his Austin Seven makes a beeline for Clapham Road. (D.A.Thompson)

42.   We now travel south by Feltham tram past Balham Station in the direction of Tooting Broadway. One form of idle speculation is to wonder what might have happened if London's tramways had been modernised, as they were in many of our European neighbours. There seems plenty room here for loading islands and a segregated right of way for trams. (D.A.Thompson)

43.   Car 1846 has just passed under the 630/612 trolleybus wires at Tooting Broadway. The track layout here was convoluted, to say the least, and it took a skilled motorman to maintain momentum across the many 'dead' sections in the conduit. (D.A.Thompson)

──────► 44.   As is well known, Tooting Broadway tube station is situated on the Northern Line to Morden. A somewhat slower way of getting to central London is represented by car 1571 on service 20 to Victoria. (LCC Tramways Trust)

──────► 45.   I quote directly from the photographer's notes: 'Car 195 held at traffic lights after leaving Defoe Road terminus, Tooting, Saturday afternoon, 21st October 1950. RT type bus on near side.' (E.Course)

←————— 46.   The change pit from conduit to overhead trolley operation was situated very close to the county boundary at the foot of Tooting High Street. This was the original meeting point of the LCC conduit tramways and the London United line from Kingston and Wimbledon. Car 1846 is bound for Stockwell Station. (E.Course)

←————— 47.   The terminus of services 2/4 at Wimbledon contained a scissors crossover, hence both these trams should be able to manoeuvre themselves forward without many problems. Trolleybus wires indicate the presence of the connecting route to Kingston and Hampton Court. (A.J.Watkins)

48.   The tramway link between Tooting and Streatham utilised Southcroft Road and Mitcham Lane. In the latter were two stretches of single track, one of which is depicted here. Aside from the rumble of the approaching tram by Ambleside Avenue, it was certainly quiet in South London when this view was taken. (D.A.Thompson)

49.　　The 'main line' from London to Croydon was joined at Streatham, St.Leonard's Church. Car 1908 awaits the green light to continue towards Purley. (D.A.Thompson)

→ 50.　　On a gloomy day, car 1365 is caught on camera at Streatham Hill Station. Many readers will remember the Express Dairy cafes with their dark blue and white décor. A tea or a luncheon would probably cost less than two shillings (10p)! (K.G.Harvie)

→ 51.　　Tram tracks were never realigned in parts of Streatham where the carriageway had been widened. On the plus side this did allow the construction of the loading island pictured in this view. Feltham cars 2080 and 2147 look suitably imposing – kings of the road, indeed! (A.J.Watkins)

52. Streatham, Telford Avenue Depot forms the backdrop to this prewar view of car 1766. In the 1930s when London Transport got the trolleybus bug really badly, it is surprising that the powers that be allocated funds for the reconditioning of trams like 1766. (R.Mayes/Terry Russell)

53. Tram service 10 and bus route 59 paralleled one another for some distance. Here an E/3 class tram and an STL bus battle it out to see who reaches the next stop first. During wartime fuel restrictions many routes such as the 59 were curtailed so that passengers were obliged to use electric traction. This was a sensible use of scarce resources. (N.Rayfield)

54. In Brixton by Gresham Road cars on service 34 'shot the plough' at the change pit and switched to the overhead. Car 1887 was reconditioned by London Transport in December 1936. It was one of the few HR/2 trams to be so treated. It was withdrawn in April 1952. Here it waits to start off in the direction of Camberwell Green. (D.A.Thompson)

55.   Coldharbour Lane, Loughborough Junction was in many respects a typical South London tramscape. Small local shops, a road devoid of traffic and the two railway bridges lend atmosphere to this view. Unfortunately, service 34's days are well and truly numbered. A temporary 'dolly stop' has appeared on the pavement. This normally indicated the imminent conversion to buses, which, in this case, occurred on 30th September 1950. (A.J.Watkins)

Sf 2036

21G   L.T.

Chge Bricklayers Arms
Tower Bridge
Chge Camberwell Grn
Boro' Station
York Road or
          The Cut
Elephant and
          Castle
Change at Catford
Dulwich Library
Forest Hill Station or
          Crofton Park Station
Blythe
          Vale
Chge New X Gate or Marq
Borough Stn. Elephant or
          Kennington Gate
Chge Clock Tower, Lew.
Rye Lane or Canal Bridge
Queens Rd. Stn. or Railway
          Bridge Old Kent Road

Transfers Issued UP

3	46 52 54	13
4		12
5	3d Single	11
6		10
7	Issued subject to the bye-laws conditions and regulations of the Board in force at the time of issue.	9a
8		9

Qh 0247

34H London Transport Trams

Chg. Embankment
Angel, Islington
Farringdon Road
(Rosebery Avenue)   72
Embankment
Change Elephant or
Camberwell Green   66
Embankment   Ex
Waterloo Station or
Bricklayers Arms
York Road or
          The Cut   3d
Boro' Station or   Single
Regency Street
Elephant
          & Castle
Og New X Gt or Marq
Kennington The Horns
Chge Clock Twr. Lew.
Railway Bg. O. Kent Rd.
Canal
          Bridge

2		10
3		9a
4		9
5		8
6		7

Lc 1492

21H   L.T. Trams

3	2½d	23
4	Workman	22
5	Return	21
6	46 52	20
7	54	19
8		18
9		17
9a		16
10	For conditions see back	15
11		14
12		13

AG 2631

21G   L.T. Trams

Change at Southwark St.
Wandsworth
          High Street   5d
Change Bricklayers Arms
Greenwich Church   SGL8
          via Deptford
Change Kennington Gate
Southcroft Rd. via Clapham
or Tooting Edy via Brixton

3		15
4	46	14
5	52	13
6	54	12
7		11
8	For con-	10
9	ditions see back	9a

CROYDON

56. A rather quaint looking Croydon car 373 represents the early London Transport era. The decision makers at 55, Broadway were sometimes forced to make do and mend older vehicles so that the service could be maintained until sufficient 'standard' cars became available to replace veterans like 373. (A.J.Watkins/ H.Wightman)

57. Car 997 is seen at Mitcham Fair Green on 4th October 1936. These tracks formerly belonged to the South Metropolitan Company and they were used in London Transport days primarily by service 30 cars working from West Croydon across South West and West London as far as Harlesden. Trolleybus conversion in the shape of route 630 happened on 12th September 1937. (H.F.Wheeller/R.S.Carpenter)

58.   At Crown Hill, Croydon, car 2128 negotiates the single track section opposite the venerable Whitgift Hospital on the right. This bottleneck was never sorted out during the life of the trams. After tramway abandonment the properties on the left of the picture were demolished. Eventually, all through traffic was banned and the area became a pedestrian precinct. Modern cars of Croydon Tramlink now cross in front of where car 2128 is standing. (K.G.Harvie)

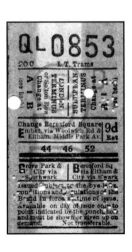

59.   At the Coombe Road crossover, South End, Croydon, by the splendidly named Ebbutts Depositories, the crew of car 375 make ready for the return journey to Thornton Heath on service 42. The first generation of Croydon trams ceased on 7th April 1951. This could well be a last day scene. (Terry Russell)

60.   Car 181 is depicted reversing on the crossover on Brighton Road outside Purley Depot. One hopes that the approaching bus driver in his brand new RT is aware of the motorman's intended direction. (K.G.Harvie)

61. Putting the trolley on the wire first time was an art that many tram conductors mastered. Of course, it was difficult at night and in the fog.

62. The Feltham cars were well suited to the straight, level Brighton Road from Croydon to Purley. Here at Purley Congregational Church, former LUT Feltham car 363, now LT car 2132, is pursued by a sister vehicle. Car 2132 was later sold to Leeds, where it received the fleet number 569. (K.G.Harvie)

SOUTH EAST LONDON

63. Coldharbour Lane forms a link between the London SW and SE postal districts. The locals were certainly well provided with public transport. This view probably dates from the summer of 1950. (N.Rayfield)

64. On a gloomy, misty South London day we observe car 1993, bravely representing electric traction despite being surrounded by members of London Transport's bus fleet. The location is Norwood Depot. The waste ground at the side was being used by LT as a temporary bus storage area. Ironically, this site was never used by the buses that replaced the local tram services. Norwood Depot closed completely on 5th April 1952. (R.Hubble)

65. Car 181 is on the approach to West Norwood terminus. For those of broader transport interests the two buses in the scene are RTL 735 on route 196 and RT 230 on route 68. (N.Rayfield)

66.   Wednesday, 9th January 1952 dawned bright and sunny, thus tempting out the photographer to capture on film this view of car 1996 at West Norwood. As can be seen, the tram occupied a single track stub in the middle of Norwood High Street. Service 33 provided a useful cross London link; its northern terminus was at Manor House. Of course, there was also the added excitement for younger passengers of the ride through the Kingsway Tram Subway. (E.Course)

→ 67.   Camberwell Green was usually a hub of tram activity. Some 250 cars an hour would pass through at peak times. A line of taxis shares the roadway with car 1880, outbound to Peckham Rye. The shelter in the centre of the picture was often used by tram devotees during inclement weather. They would break their journey here and enjoy the passing spectacle of tens of tramcars – happy days, indeed! (A.J.Watkins)

→ 68.   All traffic at this junction was controlled by temporary police lights. The motorman of car 1968 checks to see if it is safe to proceed on this part of his journey to Highgate in North London. (A.J.Watkins)

69. A great favourite with all enthusiasts was the four track layout on the splendidly named Dog Kennel Hill. The regulations stated that no two trams could occupy the same track on the hill. Trams operating along this stretch were of the HR/2 class, equipped with four motors and powerful brakes. (A.J.Watkins)

——→ 70. After grappling with the dramatic slopes of the Dulwich Hills the end of the line at Peckham Rye was a complete contrast. In this leafy, suburban backwater basking in the pleasant midday sunshine, the only sounds to disturb the tranquillity are the arrival of a tram on service 84 and the departure of the local bus. (A.J.Watkins)

Ht 7460

15J London Transport Trams

3	Blackfriars (John Carpenter St.)	3 4	
4	The Cut	Kings Rd (Chelsea)	17
5	Elephant & Castle	Parkgate Road	16
6	Camberwell Gate	Latchmere Hotel	15
7	CAMBERWELL GREEN	Clapham Junction	14
8	Loughboro' Junction	Queens-town Rd. (Lavender Hill)	13
9	Brixton Rd. (Gresham Rd)	Clapham Common Station	12
10	Stockwell Station	Clapham North Stn.	11

1d, 2d, 1d Child conditions see back

Ni 2602

15J London Transport Trams

3	Blackfriars (John Carpenter St.)	3 4	
4	The Cut	Kings Rd (Chelsea)	17
5	Elephant & Castle	Parkgate Road	16
6	Camberwell Gate	Latchmere Hotel	15
7	CAMBERWELL GREEN	Clapham Junction	14
8	Loughboro' Junction	Queens-town Rd. (Lavender Hill)	13
9	Brixton Rd. (Gresham Rd)	Clapham Common Station	12
10	Stockwell Station	Clapham North Stn.	11

For conditions see back 1d, 2d, 1d Child

HP 0068

160 L.T. Trams

London Terminus or Spion Kop
Change at B·A

Suburban Terminus
I.C.C. area Change at B·A (see back)

Change at Beresford Sq. Embankment or City and Abbey Wood Ch. Marquis Grove Park & Beresford Sq.

Change at Beresford Sq. Eltham Middle Park Ave. & Embankment

G

Embankment and Abbey Wood Routes 35 or Beresford Square or Woolwich Lane Route 44

36 38 40 ... 9d Rtn.

Not available on trolleybuses

NOT TRANSFERABLE
For conditions see back

E 2366

B London Transport Tram

London Terminus or Spion Kop
Change at A·I·B (see back)

Suburban Terminus Lewisham H.I. Stn. (via Lewisham) L.C.C. area Change at A·I·B (see back)

Change Beresford Sq. Embkt. via Woolwich Rd (from Eltham) or City from Abbey Wood
Change at Catford or Clock Tower Lew'hm
Blackwall Tunnel (from Grove Park)

E
E
B

Change at Beresford Sq. Eltham, Middle Park Av. from Emk. via Wo'w'h Rd

6d Sgl A

NEW X AND ABBEY WOOD DEPOTS

Abbey Wood (from City) or

LONDON TERMINUS		SUBURBAN TERMINUS
New Cross Gate	N	Beresford Square B
Lee Road	L	Eltham High Street E

For conditions see back.

71.　　On the afternoon of Saturday, 8th September 1951, Dr Edwin Course was on a mission to photograph Forest Hill Station. The first of his two tramway subjects focussed on car 1890. Here it is pursued by car 151. (E.Course)

72.　　On the either side of the station we encounter car 1423 at the terminus in Perry Vale. This was a conveniently situated siding off the 'main line' in Waldram Park Road. Trams could lay over here without interfering with trunk service 58 cars. (E.Course)

⟶ 73.　　Heavy tramway traffic used the road between Camberwell Green and New Cross. In one of Don Thompson's splendidly observed scenes, car 1922 passes the disused siding at the entrance to Harders Road, Peckham. The dead hand of modern town planning, in the shape of demolition and road widening, has since rendered this scene totally unrecognisable. (D.A.Thompson)

74.   The other main tramway approach to New Cross was via the Old Kent Road. Old Kent Road Station was closed in 1917 and is featured in Middleton Press album *South London Line*. Of the two surviving forms of public transport, car 176 and tram service 38 will both be withdrawn on London's last tram day, 5th July 1952. As for bus route 21 - at the time of writing it is still going strong, although RT 1264 has since been replaced by more modern vehicles. (R.Hubble)

75.   The triangular junction at New Cross Gate merited the services of a pointsman. His small canvas hut can be seen on the right of the picture. Car 1557 is on service 74 to Blackfriars. (A.J.Watkins)

76.   Also pictured at New Cross Gate is HR/2 car 1863. The tram has already 'lost' its side destination boards, and it is more than likely that this is a last day view. This vehicle perished in August 1952 in the scrap yard inferno at Penhall Road, Charlton.

77.   New Cross Depot was one of the largest in Western Europe. Thirty-six parallel tracks could accommodate 326 trams. A lone flagman stands outside the depot entrance. His job was to warn other road traffic of the frequent departures and arrivals at the depot. (A.J.Watkins)

78.   Services 36/38, 44 and 46 were often operated by trams from the former municipal fleets at East Ham and West Ham. Car 335 was once owned by the latter. We see it here outside New Cross Station. (A.J.Watkins)

79. At the Marquis of Granby trams heading for Greenwich, Woolwich and Abbey Wood diverged from those bound for Lewisham, Brockley, Grove Park, Lee Green and Woolwich via Eltham. In those days one police constable on point duty directed the traffic including a contemporay Vauxhall. (K.G.Harvie)

80. The reconstruction of the swing bridge over Deptford Creek in 1949 came as a distinct embarrassment to London Transport. They had hoped to get rid of the trams before the old bridge gave up the ghost. As it was, the new 'temporary' structure and its associated trackwork immediately proved a magnet for tram fans. A tram is depicted crossing the temporary lifting bridge. (A.J.Watkins)

81. On the Greenwich side of Creek Bridge we observe car 591. The 500 series E/1 cars were often to be seen on services 68/70. They were slow, but few seemed to mind as they trundled sedately out of Greenwich and past the docks. (A.J.Watkins)

82. In theory there was a regulation limiting the number of trams standing at the terminus in Greenwich, Church Street, however, it certainly was not being enforced when Alan Watkins took this view. Heading the queue is car 916. This vehicle was scrapped in October 1951. (A.J.Watkins)

83. Nelson Street in 2006 looks very much as it did in this photo. Obviously, the modern era has brought a vast influx of traffic plus a one way scheme, but this part of Greenwich really hasn't changed that markedly. The last tram ran here on 5th July 1952. (A.J.Watkins)

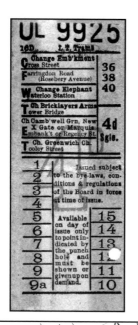

UL 9925

19D — L.T. Trams

Change Emb'kment	
Cross Street	
Farringdon Road	36
(Rosebery Avenue)	38
Change Elephant	40
Waterloo Station	
Ch Bricklayers Arms	
Tower Bridge	
Ch Camb'well Grn, New	4d
X Gate or Marquis	Sgle.
Embank't or Regency St.	
Ch. Greenwich Ch.	
Tooley Street	

1	Issued subject	
2	to the bye-laws, con-	
3	ditions & regulations	
4	of the Board in force	
	at time of issue.	
5	Available	15
6	on day of	14
7	issue only	13
	to point in-	
8	dicated by	12
	the punch	
9	hole and	11
	must be	
9a	shown or	10
	given up on	
	demand.	

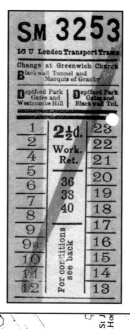

SM 3253

16 U London Transport Trams

Change at Greenwich Church
Blackwall Tunnel and
Marquis of Granby

Deptford Park	Deptford Park
Gates and	Gates and
Westcombe Hill	Blackwall Tnl.

1	2½d.	23
2	Work.	22
4	Ret.	21
5		20
6	36	19
7	38	18
8	40	17
9		16
9a		16
10		15
11	For conditions	14
12	see back	13

Jb 8445

219 — L.T. Trams

Chge Bricklayers Arms	
Tower Bridge	
Chge Camberwell Grn	
Boro' Station	
York Road or	
The Cut	
Elephant and	
Castle	
Change at Catford	
Dulwich Library	
Forest Hill Station or	
Crofton Park Station	
Blythe	
Vale	
Chg New X Gate or Marq	
Borough Stn., Elephant or	
Kennington Gate	
Chge Clock Tower, Dew	
Rye Lane or Canal Bridge	
Queens Rd. Stn. or Railway	
Bridge Old Kent Road	

Transfers Issued UP

3	46 52 54	13
4		12
5	3d Single	11
6		10
7	Issued subject	9a
8	to the bye-laws,	9
	conditions and	
	regulations of	
	the Board in	
	force at the	
	time of issue.	

Service 58 traversed many typical South London streets as well as the four track Dog Kennel Hill. However, on Lewisham Road, Blackheath Hill the tramway was definitely more 'municipal' than 'metropolitan'. A beautiful canopy of trees once framed the single track and loops layout. The area was surveyed by Ordnance Survey in September 1949 and the sheet was published in 1950. These maps, produced to a scale of 1:1250, were the last to feature the tramway track layout of the first generation system.

← 84. We are looking south along Lewisham Road, at the corner of Morden Hill, where the double track ended. Car 1400 was the Charlton Works staff car from April to September 1951. From the length of the shadows it would seem that it has a cargo of homeward bound workers. (D.A.Thompson)

← 85. Car 1859 is depicted in Lewisham Road opposite the post box at the entrance to Blackheath Rise. This location can be easily identified on the accompanying map. (K.G.Harvie)

86. Blackwall Lane leads into Tunnel Avenue and once boasted a double track conduit tramway. Car 1897 has not long left the terminus outside the southern entrance to Blackwall Tunnel. The area has since been transformed by motorway approach roads and the Millennium Dome. (R.Hubble)

←———— 87. Woolwich Road, Charlton only really came to life on match days, when Charlton Athletic were playing at home. Spectators at The Valley, which had a capacity of 70,000 in those days, would be catered for by an intensive tram service. In quieter times car 593 is seen near Charlton Church Lane. (K.G.Harvie)

←———— 88. Car 175 is about to forsake the conduit for the overhead. It follows a 696 trolleybus, which is on a short working to Welling Corner. The two trolleybus routes 696 and 698 were isolated from the rest of the London system. They were both replaced by buses on 3rd March 1959. (J.Wills)

89. No book on the trams of South London would be complete without a view of Beresford Square, Woolwich Market. Trams, buses, trolleybuses, motor cars, delivery vans, horse drawn carts and shoppers all mingled freely. The square still exists, although it is now bypassed by through traffic and the tram rails, which outlived the trams themselves by several decades, have now disappeared.

90.   The restricted width of Bostall Hill, Plumstead merited a single track layout. The one passing place was at the entrance to Woodhurst Road. Car 1510 waits for its turn to proceed towards Abbey Wood. In the summer of 1935 the overhead wiring was already being altered for the introduction, later in the year, of the new trolleybuses on route 698. (G.N.Southerden)

91.   On the crown of Basildon Road, where it meets Bostall Hill, standard E/1 car 1568 takes on passengers. Note the separate overhead wires for trams and trolleybuses. This arrangement speeded up the service, when a tram wished to overtake a 698 trolleybus. (A.J.Watkins)

92.   Abbey Wood was one of the most photographed tram termini in London. This classic view by Alan Watkins of car 1597 is one of the best. (A.J.Watkins)

93.   We look due east to the Harrow Inn on the corner of Knee Hill and Abbey Road. The tram has just left Abbey Wood Depot on service 46. The car will travel via Woolwich, Eltham, Lewisham and New Cross to reach the City terminus at Southwark Bridge. The fare for the whole journey was seven old pence! (A.J.Watkins)

94.   Abbey Wood Depot, situated at the far extremity of the system within yards of the Kentish boundary, was once described by a famous tram aficionado as 'a jolly place, full of jolly people operating jolly trams'. This statement, worthy of John Betjeman, omits to record the fact that the depot once housed 56 trams for the local services. Like almost all of London's tramway heritage it was subsequently demolished. The site now houses a somewhat less jolly block of flats! (A.J.Watkins)

95.   Knee Hill, Abbey Wood was also the short lived terminus of service 98 to Belvedere, Erith and Bexleyheath. This was replaced by trolleybus route 698 on 10th November 1935. In what could well be the summer of 1935, the driver of former Erith car 13D answers a query from a member of the public. The point iron will cause 13D to take the connecting rails into Abbey Road. This actual link between the former Erith and LCC system was constructed by LT in December 1933.

96.   The tramway between Woolwich and Eltham was opened in 1910, and later extended to Lee Green to meet the tracks from Lewisham. Former East Ham car 96 is seen at Eltham Well Hall Station. Nowadays the area in the foreground forms part of a bridge over the Rochester Way Relief Road; Well Hall Station has been moved and renamed. (D.A.Thompson)

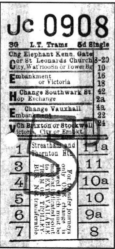

⟶ 97.   Car 295 takes the sharp bend outside St.John's Church, Eltham. On the final day of the system trams were often filled to capacity with folk wanting to take one nostalgic last trip. In an attempt to introduce more flexibility into the service, the car following 295 will reverse at Eltham Church to return to New Cross Depot. (R.Hubble)

98.   The main service through Eltham to the City was numbered 46; however, cars working from Woolwich to Eltham Green retained the original 44 service number. Car 304 slows for the roundabout at the Yorkshire Grey. Eltham Hill looks prime tramway operating territory – ample width roadway with little other traffic. In the early 1960s it was rebuilt into a dual carriageway. (R.Hubble)

99.   We observe the change pit outside Lee Green Fire Station, as it looked on 10th May 1952. The conductor of the tram on the extreme left of the view will shortly lower the trolley pole and the car will move off, taking power from the conduit. Meanwhile, car 1871, with pole raised, ejects its conduit plough and continues along Eltham Road. (J.C.Gillham)

100.   Former   Walthamstow car 2049 was transferred from Streatham to New Cross on 1st October 1950. At Lee Green the motorman has just made a 'pit stop' and is now rejoining his vehicle. (K.G.Harvie)

101. South of Catford, the London County Council built several large housing estates. These were served by a new tramway running through Downham to Grove Park. Car 563 is in Bromley Road. (D.A.Thompson) ——————➤ 102. The change pit was situated at the western end of Downham Way. Car 1841 is about to move off the conduit and on to the overhead trolley section. (A.J.Watkins)

——————➤ 103. We end our tour of South London's tramways on a sunny day at Grove Park. Car 582 is about to return to Southwark Bridge on service 52. (A.J.Watkins)

TRAMS AND TRACKWORK

104.   The conductor of car 578 is obviously concerned about an imminent dewirement. Luckily, here at Beresford Square he does have the time and space to alert the motorman so that they can sort things out. Trams were often shunted at this location in order to allow late running cars to make up time. (K.G.Harvie)

──────→ 105. More serious faults than a dewired trolley might require the assistance of a breakdown tender. Feltham car 2102 has encountered difficulties and is now relying on a push to return to the depot. A fitter and an inspector look on. (A.J.Watkins)

──────→ 106.   The crew of LT service vehicle 75Q are being given last minute instructions at Lee Green. Although primarily for use on overhead equipped lines, this vehicle also contained tools for effecting repairs to damaged ploughs and for checking conduit faults. (A.J.Watkins)

107.   The repair and installation of new rails was a continuous process. In this evocative view at the corner of Victoria Embankment and Blackfriars Bridge the granite setts have been removed to expose the conduit track. Note the old fashioned tar boiler in the background. (A.J.Watkins)

108.   The new layout by County Hall attracted many photographers. We see the heavy yokes needed to support the conduit and the running rails. This westbound single track had a very short life. It opened on 12th October 1950 and was closed on 5th July 1952. (A.J.Watkins)

109. Our final track view shows the beautifully symmetrical design of a trailing conduit crossover. The location is Great Dover Street and the tram is an ex-East Ham car, now masquerading as LT car 83. (Terry Russell)

110. Car 1400 is depicted in prewar guise at Kennington. This vehicle was involved in the partial modernisation programme of 1935-1937. For many they were known as 'rehabilitated trams' or simply 'rehabs'.

111. Rehab 1502 was one of the first ones to be treated in November 1935. It was photographed early in its 'reconditioned life'. It was withdrawn from service in October 1951. (Terry Russell)

⟶ Car Plan of 1622, as now preserved at the National Tramway Museum, and featured on the back cover.

112. This prewar scene is included for its rarity value. Apart from the seldom photograph 16A service number, the tram itself is of interest. This vehicle, car 1038, was one of the prototypes for the rehab scheme. It entered Charlton Works in the autumn of 1934 to re-emerge in January 1935. (Terry Russell)

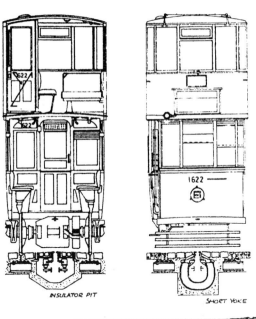

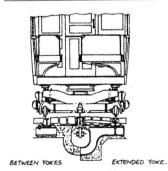

THE FOLLOWING FINE SCALE 'O' GAUGE
PARTS ARE AVAILABLE :- MOTORED TRUCKS,
STAIRS, SEATS, CONTROLLERS, LIFEGUARDS,
BRAKES, FOGLAMPS & PLOUGH CARRIER.
SEND SAE. TO TERRY RUSSELL FOR LIST.

LONDON TRANSPORT
DOUBLE DECK TRAM

TYPE : EX L.C.C. CLASS E1 REBUILT	SCALE : 4 mm = 1 Foot

DRAWING No. TC 75

INSULATOR PIT

SHORT YOKE

BETWEEN YOKES

EXTENDED YOKE.

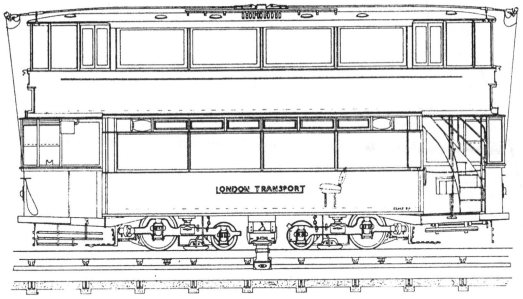

LONDON TRANSPORT

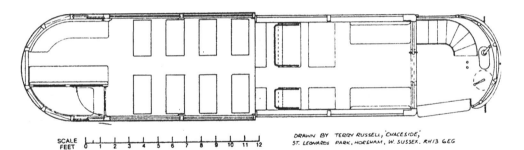

SCALE
FEET 0 1 2 3 4 5 6 7 8 9 10 11 12

DRAWN BY TERRY RUSSELL, 'CHACESIDE',
ST. LEONARDS PARK, HORSHAM, W. SUSSEX. RH13 6EG

THIS CAR IS BEING RESTORED BY THE L.C.C. TRAMWAY TRUST.

113.   Car 1191 is pictured nearing the end of its life. It has already sustained some damage to the dash. It was withdrawn in September 1950. (A.J.Watkins)

114.   This was the standard of comfort offered on the lower deck of car 559. Note the upholstered 2+1 transverse seating; of course, all these seats could be flipped over when the tram reversed. This view was taken on the last day of operation.   (J.C.Gillham)

115.   This is the top deck of rehab car 1386. Passengers on the end seats by the upper deck stairway bulkhead had a splendid panorama of the road ahead.   (J.C.Gillham)

116. Passengers using the stairs had this view of the end platform. Note the controller handle. This straightforward device controlled the speed and braking of the tram. Much of the tram driver's day was spent in applying the Power and Coast technique – this saved energy and obviously could not be employed on the replacing buses. (A.J.Watkins)

117. The standard London tram ran on eight wheels grouped into two bogies. Each maximum traction bogie (as illustrated here) had two large wheels, powered by an electric motor, and two smaller 'pony wheels'. HR/2 class cars, built for tackling Dog Kennel Hill, had two equal wheel bogies and four traction motors. (A.J.Watkins)

FINALE

118. Car 1931 can actually lay claim to be the last service tram to enter Penhall Road yard at 3.35am on Sunday, 6th July 1952. On the previous day it was hired by the Light Railway Transport League for a farewell tour. It is depicted here manoeuvring at Beresford Square. Trolleybus 799B on route 696 is trying to squeeze past. (K.G.Harvie)

IN PIOUS MEMORY

OF

LONDON'S LAST TRAMCAR

WHICH PASSED AWAY

ON THE 5ᴛʜ JULY 1952

Et fumus ejus ascendet . . .

This commemorative piece was printed by Saint Gregory's Press for the late Father Benedict Sankey. The text is 10 and 12 point Caslon Old Face, with various brass rules for the top and bottom adornments. Notice that Father Benedict has resisted the temptation to use Sic Transit Gloria Mundi as his Latin tag!

119.   This is home ground for your author. At the Welcome Inn tram stop in Well Hall Road, he first encountered the wonderful red and cream tramcars. With only a few hours to run, car 1858 passes the Cosy Café on the corner of Dunblane Road. The Cosy Café was a favourite with tram crews, and it was here that they used to top up their tea cans. The café now belongs firmly to the past, but a farsighted gentleman, named P.J.Davis, purchased car 1858 from London Transport and the vehicle now runs at the East Anglia Transport Museum at Carlton Colville near Lowestoft. (R.Hubble)

120.   The trams have come to the end of their journey and this sad sight of track removal was repeated all over South London. As if to emphasis the changing times, replacing buses drive past on the adjacent carriageway in Bromley Road. (R.Hubble)

MP Middleton Press

EVOLVING THE ULTIMATE RAIL ENCYCLOPEDIA

Easebourne Lane, Midhurst, West Sussex.
GU29 9AZ   Tel:01730 813169

www.middletonpress.co.uk   email:info@middletonpress.co.uk

A-0 906520   B-1 873793   C-1 901706   D-1 904474

OOP Out of print at time of printing - Please check availability   BROCHURE AVAILABLE SHOWING NEW TITLES